GET WELL SOON

Cold

Anita Ganeri and

Beatriz Castro

Enslow PUBLISHING

Published in 2025 by Enslow Publishing, LLC
2544 Clinton Street
Buffalo, NY 14224

First published in Great Britain in 2023 by Hodder & Stoughton

Series editor: Julia Bird
Illustrator: Beatriz Castro
Design: Collaborate

Manufactured in the United States of America

CPSIA compliance information: Batch #CSENS25: For further information contact Enslow Publishing LLC, New York, New York at 1-800-398-2504.

Please visit our website, www.enslowpublishing.com. For a free color catalog of all our high-quality books, call toll free 1-800-398-2504 or fax 1-877-980-4454.

Cataloging-in-Publication Data

Names: Ganeri, Anita, 1961-. | Castro, Beatriz.
Title: Cold / by Anita Ganeri and Beatriz Castro.
Description: Buffalo, NY : Enslow Publishing, 2025. | Series: Get well soon
Identifiers: ISBN 9781978538597 (pbk.) | ISBN 9781978538603 (library bound) |
ISBN 9781978538610 (ebook)
Subjects: LCSH: Cold (Disease)--Juvenile literature. |
Cold (Disease)--Prevention--Juvenile literature.
Classification: LCC RF361.G24 2025 | DDC 616.2'05--dc23

Find us on

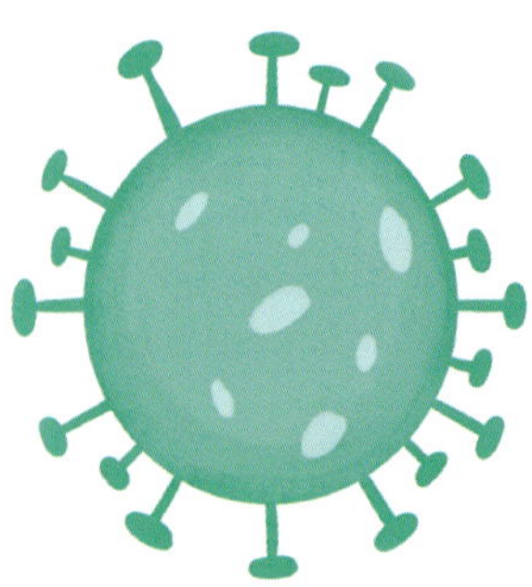

GET WELL SOON

Cold

Hello there. My name is Roshan, and this book is all about the time I caught a cold. I felt really terrible. My nose was all blocked up. I had a sore throat and I couldn't stop sneezing. But after a few days' rest, I felt much better.

This book has lots of information and advice about catching a cold to help you and your parents or caregivers. You can find out:

What is a cold?

How do you catch one?

Why does a cold make you sneeze?

What makes you feel better?

This book is about an illness called the common cold. You might catch three or more colds a year. And you're not alone. At any time, millions of people around the world have a cold!

It's Thursday morning. Roshan and his friends are standing outside school. Today is the day of the school trip to the science museum. They are waiting for the bus.

The children have been looking forward to this trip for weeks. They all start talking about what they want to see.

A few minutes later, the bus drives into the parking lot.
The children's chatter gets louder and louder.
Miss Lindsay, the class teacher, claps her hands.

Miss Lindsay and her teaching assistant,
Mr. Balik, count the children as they
climb on board the bus.

Roshan is lining up with his partner, Poppy. He isn't feeling very well. He has a sore throat and a headache.

At the science museum, the children are amazed by all the different things on display.

In the space display, Tom spots a space suit.

Sophia rushes straight to the dinosaurs.

Meanwhile, Roshan heads towards the flight simulator, where he can pretend to fly a jet.

This was meant to be the best part of the trip. Roshan wants to be a pilot when he grows up. But his headache is getting worse, and his legs are aching. He decides to sit down for a moment.

Then Roshan hears Miss Lindsay's voice.

The class gathers around Miss Lindsay. She points to a display about germs.

Some facts about germs ...

Germs are so tiny you need a microscope to see them.

Germs are everywhere – in the air, in the soil, and on the things around you.

The smallest germs are called viruses.

There are thousands of different kinds of germs.

Viruses can get inside your body through your eyes, nose, or mouth.

Your body usually fights germs off, but sometimes they make you sick.

Here are some of the illnesses that are caused by viruses:

COMMON COLD

* A common illness of your nose and throat
* Spread by air in tiny droplets
* Symptoms include: coughing. sneezing, sore throat

INFLUENZA

* A more serious illness, also known as the "flu" for short
* Spread by air in tiny droplets
* Symptoms include: fever, muscle aches, feeling exhausted

CHICKENPOX

* A less common illness, because most kids in the U.S. are vaccinated against it
* Spread by air in tiny droplets.
* Symptoms include: fever, itchy spots on the skin

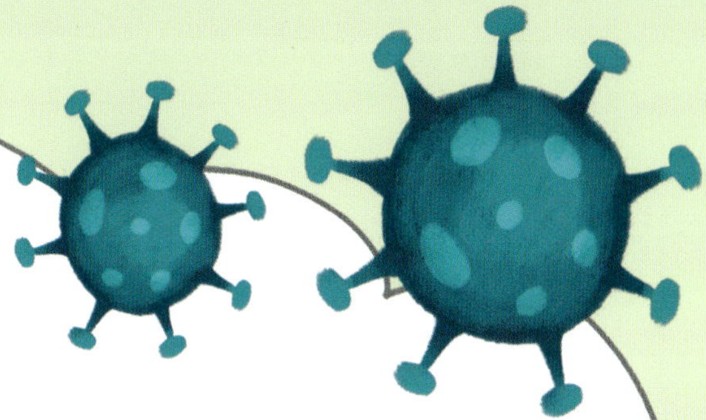

COVID-19

* A serious new disease
* Spread through the air and by touching contaminated surfaces
* Symptoms include: a continuous cough, high temperature, and loss or change to senses of taste and smell.

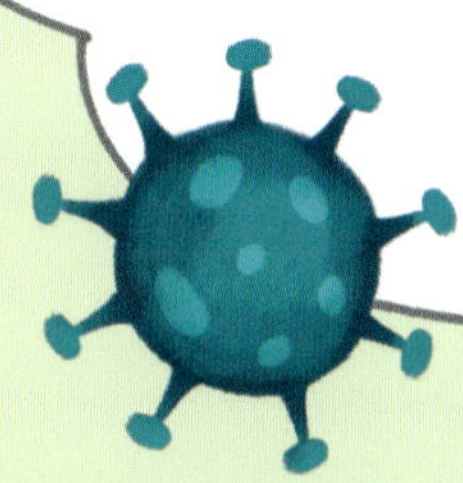

VACCINES

Vaccines are medicines that help stop you from getting infections.

When you get a vaccine, it teaches your body how to fight off the germ. If the germ tries to infect you later, your body is ready to fight it off before it makes you sick.

Every year, vaccines save millions of lives around the world.

Later, back at school, the class settles down at their tables. Roshan is feeling very sleepy. He's finding it difficult to concentrate.

Suddenly, there's a loud noise ...

Roshan has made a great big snotty sneeze!

The children sitting nearby quickly lean away from poor Roshan, but Mr. Balik smiles sympathetically.

Roshan finally gets it – he has caught a cold!

COLD CLUES

Colds are very common illnesses. Adults can catch around 2 to 3 colds a year; children may catch even more. Right now, millions of people around the world have got a cold!

Your body makes slimy mucus to trap the germs.

But the mucus and swelling block up your breathing tubes.

You sneeze and cough to try to clear the blockages.

When you sneeze or cough, you blast thousands of tiny droplets of mucus into the air. If other people breathe these droplets in, they could catch the cold too.

Be sure to sneeze into a tissue or cover your mouth when you cough. That will help stop the germs from spreading.

Roshan's dad comes to pick him up at the end of school. Roshan is sneezing a lot now. His throat is sore, and he keeps coughing.

Back home, Dad sends Roshan straight to bed.

Later, he brings Roshan his favorite spicy soup. But Roshan can't taste very much.

TOP TIPS

A cold is usually a mild illness, and you don't need to see a doctor. But there are some things that can help you feel better:

1. Get plenty of rest.
2. Keep warm.
3. Drink plenty of water.
4. Eat small amounts of soup, or other food that is easy to swallow.

DID YOU KNOW?

While you have a cold, you are infectious. This means that you can easily spread your germs to other people. You can start spreading a cold a few days before you get any symptoms. You're infectious until all your symptoms are gone.

Here are some things you can do to keep your cold from spreading, and to keep yourself from catching a cold from someone else:

Put your tissues
in the trash.

Don't share towels or
things like mugs.

Try not to touch your
eyes or nose!

The next morning, Roshan is feeling a bit better.
But he's still coughing and keeps blowing his nose.

By Monday, Roshan's feeling much better. He can't wait to go back to school and see his friends. He packs plenty of tissues in his bag.

In the classroom, Roshan looks around for Tom. He can't see him anywhere. He asks Mr. Balik if he knows where Tom is.

QUIZ

Now that you've reached the end of the book, how much do you think you know about colds? Try this quick quiz to find out.

1. What causes a cold?
a) Viruses
b) Germs
c) Cold weather

2. Which of these are signs of a cold?
a) Sneezing
b) Coughing
c) Runny nose

3. Which of these stops a cold from spreading?
a) Sharing things like mugs and towels
b) Having dirty hands
c) Blowing your nose into a tissue

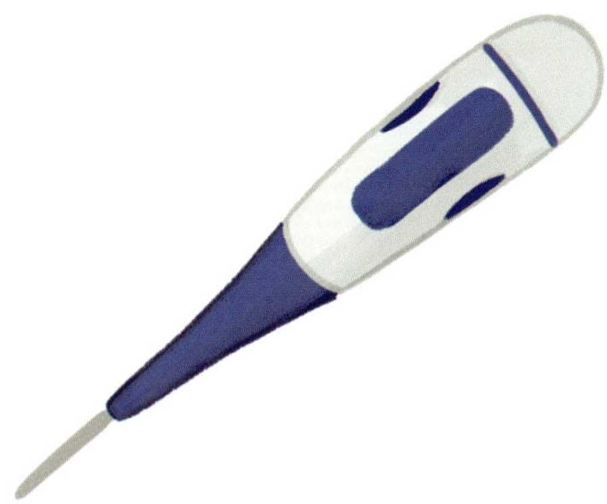

4. Which of these will help you feel better?
a) Running around
b) Jumping up and down
c) Getting plenty of rest

5. When are you no longer contagious?
a) After a week
b) After a month
c) When your symptoms are gone

Answers:
1. a) & b); 2. All of them; 3. c); 4. c); 5. c)

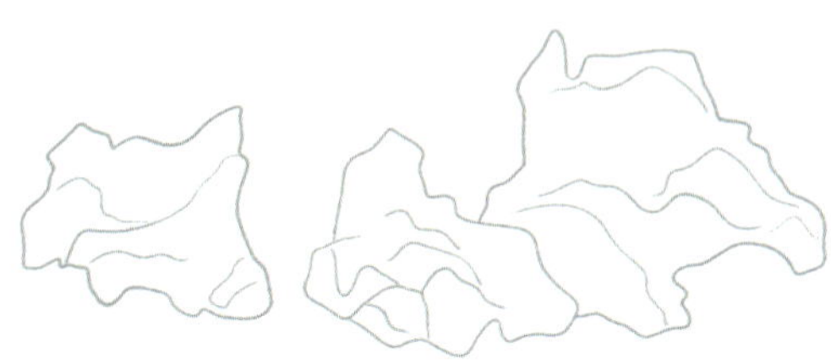

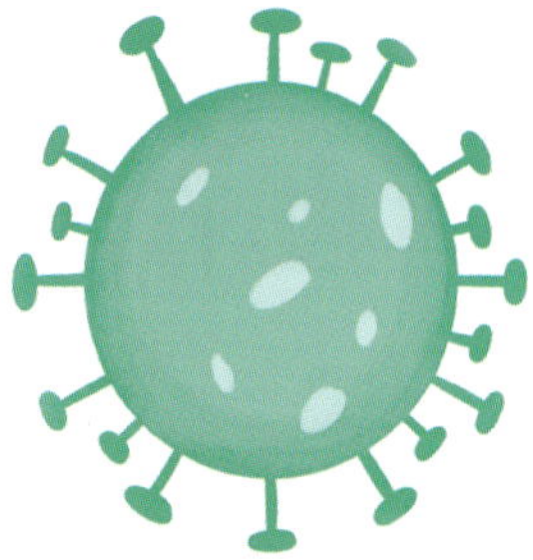

USEFUL WORDS

contaminated
Affected by germs.

droplets
Tiny drops of liquid.

germs
Tiny living things that can cause disease.

infectious
Able to cause disease by being close to someone who has it.

microscope
A scientific instrument used to make tiny objects look bigger.

mucus
Thick liquid made by your nose; also called snot.

sympathetically
In a kind and understanding way.

symptoms
Signs of an illness.

vaccines
Medicines usually given by injection to keep you from getting a disease.

viruses
Types of germs that can get inside your body and make you sick.

MORE INFORMATION

www.kidshealth.org/en/kids/colds.html
More information about catching a cold, and how to feel better.

www.kids.britannica.com/kids/article/Common-Cold/400001
Learn more about catching a cold, and how it affects your body.

BOOKS

Health and My Body: The Common Cold by Beth Bence Reinke (Pebble Books, 2021)

Tiny Science: Germs by Anna Claybourne (Gareth Stevens, 2025)

The Secret Life of Viruses: Incredible Science Facts About Germs, Vaccines and What You Can Do to Stay Healthy by Mariona Tolosa Sisteré (Sourcebooks, 2021)

ADVICE FOR PARENTS AND CAREGIVERS

Colds and the flu start off with many of the same symptoms, which makes them difficult to tell apart. But the flu is more serious than a cold, and can make your child feel really sick.

Here are some signs to look out for to tell them apart:

COLD

- A cold usually appears slowly, over a few days.
- A cold may cause a slightly raised temperature.
- A cold can make a child feel unwell, but they may be able to carry on as normal.
- A cold mainly affects the nose and throat.

FLU

- The flu can come on quickly, maybe in a few hours.
- The flu can cause a sudden high temperature of 100°F (38°C) or above.
- The flu may make a child feel so ill and tired that they have to stop all usual activities.
- The flu also affects the nose and throat, but may also cause a headache, earache, stomachache, and aching muscles.

If you think that your child has the flu, follow the tips for treating a cold (see page 23). Call your doctor if you're worried about your child or if their temperature lasts for five days or more and doesn't come down with acetaminophen.

You can also ask for advice from your pediatrician.

INDEX

coughing
4, 5, 16, 18, 20, 22, 24, 26

COVID-19
15

flu
14, 30, 31

germs
12–13, 15, 20, 21, 24

headache
9,11

mucus (snot)
16, 21

rest
23

sneezing
4, 5, 16, 19, 20, 22, 24

sore

  muscles 11

  throat 4, 9, 19, 22

symptoms
20–21, 24

temperature
30, 31

  raised 30, 31

tiredness
19

tissues
17, 21, 24, 25, 27

vaccines
15

  flu 31

viruses
13, 14–15

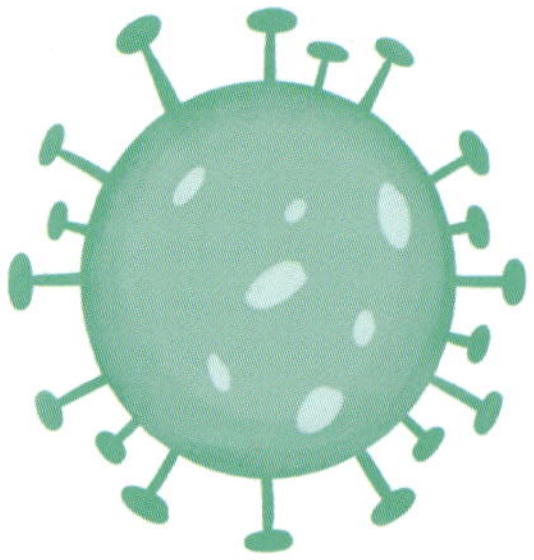